POWERFUL
or
POWERLESS

*A Spiritual, Not Religious
Look At The 12 Steps*

Georgia Prescott

Powerful or Powerless:
A Spiritual, Not Religious Look At The 12 Steps
Georgia Prescott

1275 Starboard Dr., West Sacramento, CA 95691

Visit our website at www.revgeorgia.com

Library of Congress Cataloging-in-Publication Data:(filed)

ISBN 13: 978-0-9826817-0-1

Printed in the United States of America

Book Design by Karrie Ross www.KarrieRoss.com
Symbol art on cover by Mary McCaffery
The book cover's Science of Mind Symbol is used with permission by the Centers For Spiritual Living.

First Edition: April 2010

POWERFUL
or
POWERLESS

To Donna Menzies who
inspires my life with her
love of God, love of people, and love of me.
and,
To all the sponsors on the planet who
give themselves so selflessly to carry the
message of experience, strength and hope.

My deep thanks to…

My editors Sylvia Aquino, Donna Menzies, Peggy Prescott, Donna Santiago-Woods, and Rhonda Youngblood for their great suggestions and editing skills;

To Rev. Julie Interrante, Rev. Betsy Elliot, Rev. Stephen Gilbert, Donna Santiago-Woods, Rhonda Youngblood, RScP, Peggy Tillary, RScP for the beautiful prayers in beginning of each chapter.

To Mary McCaffery for the beautiful painting of the Science of Mind symbol that hangs in my office and now is on the cover of this book.

To Alison O. and my many other sponsors who helped me to better understand the 12 Steps. To Joe and Connie who continue to inspire me by attracting so many to recovery through their authentic living of the 12 Steps. To Brynde Lambert, RScP who continues to inspire me through her commitment to New Thought teachings.

To Rev. Karyl Huntly and Rev. Mary Murray Shelton who brought New Thought teachings alive for me.

To Rosie Camarena for her creativity in creating my webpage and for keeping CSA in good order.

And finally, to Bill Wilson, Dr. Bob, Ernest Holmes, and Charles and Myrtle Fillmore. You 5 have changed the world.

Powerful or Powerless?

A Spiritual, Not Religious,
Look At The 12 Steps

Introduction

I can't tell you how many people, in just 10 years of ministry, have asked me how they can be both powerless over their addiction and also know they have the Power of God within them. They want to know how they can say they are powerful beyond measure and yet admit that booze, food, porn sites, gambling, and drugs have power over them. Some have even come into my office proudly announcing they've left AA so they can be "true to their new-found divinity."

I wrote this book to offer an opinion on how people who are recovering from addiction can use two of the most powerful movements on the planet; the New Thought movement and the Recovery movement to co-create with Spirit a life beyond our wildest dreams. They are compatible. This is not a book on how to use the 12 Steps. If you are interested in recovery through the 12 Steps, get involved in a home group and get a sponsor who has what you want. Then begin. I believe the 12 Steps are divinely inspired and they need no help from me.

So first, what is the New Thought (not New Age) Movement? Started in the late 19th Century in the United States, New Thought centers and churches focus on individual and planetary unification with a Higher Power. The unification is not something we strive for or work to make happen, it's something we strive for and work to <u>recognize.</u> We are already one with God and with each other and all sentient beings. No matter how much we've screwed up, we are still one with God. Our work is to remember that very oneness, and our recovery from addiction will help us.

In New Thought we ask ourselves to unify in consciousness with this Presence. We study the teachings of Jesus (as well as Buddha, Lao Tzu, and many earth-based and modern teachers) and are reminded of his question to the faithful, "Are ye not gods?" We believe that God's life is our life now. We understand that we are not all of God, but we believe that God is all of us. More about this in Step 3.

Folks in the New Thought movement sometimes call our Higher Power God, Allah, Elohim, The Atman/Brahman Presence, Goddess, Divine Intelligence, or Infinite Love, to name just a few. The One can be called anything because God is everything. Similar to those in AA, we have a God of our understanding and we choose the name that works for us. The first thing we do in our prayer work is to make sure we understand what God looks like to us. Have we made God in the image and likeness of our parents, teachers, clergy, or others? More about this in Step 3.

Those of us in New Thought, like folks in 12 Step programs, are willing to take 100% responsibility for our lives. We understand that even when things "happen to us" we have a spiritual choice to make the situation more painful or less painful. We also believe that we have had a hand in most of the so-called bad things that have happened to us. More about this in Step 4 and 10.

New Thought teachings invite us to take responsibility for our thoughts, recognizing that each thought is creative and influential. Notice I did not say that each thought becomes manifest. Thank God. While some thoughts may escape manifestation, none escape influencing our consciousness. In New Thought churches we say that consciousness is cause, and we're careful what we allow in. Repetitive negative thinking can set the scene for a very challenged life. We strive to keep our thoughts and comments positive, preferring to focus on what is working instead of what is not working in our life.

One of my favorite positive-talk "church stories" is about a father who gave his six- year old son, Rojelio, a plastic ball and bat to celebrate his birthday. One day the father stood at the kitchen window and watched as Rojelio threw the ball in the air, took a swing and missed. Again, he threw the ball up, took a swing and missed. Over and over again, Rojelio would throw the ball in the air, swing and miss. Finally, his dad, worried his son would get discouraged, went out and asked him how he was doing. Rojelio responded, "Oh, fine, Poppy, I'm the greatest pitcher that ever lived!" He was focusing on what worked!

We need to take care, however, not to throw recovery out the window with metaphysical bubble-headedness. Positive language is language that reflects how we feel about ourselves and only we get to define what that sounds like. Nobody else. Not your mother or your teacher or your clergy. Once, when I sat for my Practitioner (spiritual coach) panels for licensing, one of the panelists asked me to tell them a little about myself. I said I was a mother, a golfer, a CEO of a non-profit, a lesbian, and an alcoholic. I barely got the word alcoholic out of my mouth when the chair of the panel, a senior minister jumped in with, "never name and claim a disease." I wasn't entirely sure whether he was talking about the lesbian or alcoholic part, but it became clear to me in that moment, that he thought one or the other was "bad." The words addict, alcoholic, compulsive overeater that we call ourselves are only negative or "bad" words if we make them so. For every one of the self-describing adjectives I gave to the panel, I can find both "good" and "bad" connotations. It is all relative.

Being an alcoholic is the best thing that ever happened to me, and I'm proud to name and claim it. In taking my head out of the sand, in no longer pretending that everything was fine when it wasn't, I found God. I was introduced to spiritual principles in such a way that I could use them, not be beaten up by them. I was open to the message of Rev. Mary when I walked into her church. It made me who I am today, a woman who lives without daily incomprehensible demoralization.

One of the challenges for New Thought faithful in the recovery community can be dealing with what looks like negative talk in conference-approved literature and in meetings. For instance, reading the 24 Hour Book can be a hair-pulling experience for those of us being vigilant about negative self-talk. We should, however, be clear that it is possible, and maybe even helpful, for us to read it every day. My most recent sponsor "required" me to read the 24 hour book before my 30-minute meditation, which was to take place before my daily call to her at 6:30am. I complained, whined, and told her it was interfering with my religion, but nothing worked. She is a fabulous sponsor, and I didn't want to lose her so I read it. Now, the only way I could read it was to translate the language into a positive message. The work that this required anchored the message much deeper in me than if I just read it.

In short, I have to be awake and aware as I navigate the 12 Steps. Still, I recommend 12 Step Recovery to people in New Thought communities without any hesitation as a very effective method of dealing with addiction. It's not the only way, just a very effective way, and the way that saved my life.

I have included affirmative prayers at the beginning of each Step to help anchor our intention to stay true to our teachings, both our New Thought teachings and our recovery teachings. I invite you to take a moment and slowly whisper them aloud to yourself. Let each sentence sink in. The prayers affirm the Truth of your being.

At the end of each Step, I offer an affirmation to help us "speak" to any naysayers who might be lurking in our subconscious, lurking in our "internal committee". Again, I find them most helpful when read slowly and aloud. If, after you read this book, you have questions, please go to my website at Revgeorgia.com or csasacramento.org and send me an email.

Step 1

We admitted we were powerless over alcohol— that our lives had become unmanageable.

A Prayer For Step 1

*I know there is one Life. It is the Life of God.
It is the presence in all things. It is the guiding
force of the planets, nature and the entire universe and
beyond. It lives and breathes all things. There is
nothing that lives outside of the heart and life of the Divine.
In knowing this truth, I know there is nothing for me
to hang on to. There is nothing for me to figure out.
In my powerlessness over alcohol, I recognize the power of
God. I am grateful for the experience of perfect guidance and
love now. I give thanks for the perfect expression of God in
my life with each breath, each thought and each action.
I release my word and I know it is done. And so it is.*

Admitting you are powerless is the most powerful thing you will ever do and I want to discuss why in a minute, but first I want to talk about unmanageability.

Once we admit that we drink too much, it's not hard, even for those of us in New Thought, to admit that our lives have become unmanageable. Indeed many of us lost jobs, opportunities for better jobs, family, friends, our self-respect, and had come to accept the repetitive visit of incomprehensible demoralization in our lives. Maybe we are not falling down drunk every night, but we notice we are relying on a few drinks to socialize or to parent our kids or to get through that next presentation or to reward ourselves for a job well done. Although I couldn't cook much more than boxed macaroni and cheese, I once bought a restaurant because I thought Georgia O'Quiche was a fabulous name. After my two business partners of equally clear thinking and I ran the business into the ground, I was thousands of dollars in debt. And that is only one example of the unmanageability of my life.

For the most part, spiritual folks don't seem to have a problem admitting unmanageability. Maybe we were fooling others, people in our churches, synagogues, ashrams, and even family members, but we weren't fooling ourselves. We did not have a life that Spirit could use. When we embrace the teachings of New Thought wisdom, we understand we're here for a sacred purpose, and we're pretty sure that doing whatever it takes to get the next drink or cupcake or visit to a porn site isn't it.

You are a sacred being who is whole, perfect, and complete. If alcohol or any other substance is assisting you in covering the perfection that you are, your life is unmanageable. Remember, we weren't sent here to get by, to make-do, or to be part of anybody's problem. We were sent here to be a part of the solution to separation thinking! We are here to represent the Power for Good in the Universe. But often, this part of the Step is preaching to the choir. Admitting the unmanageability is the easy part.

Where I see my New Thought sisters and brothers putting on the brakes to fully embrace recovery through the 12 Steps of Alcoholics Anonymous is the idea that we are powerless over alcohol. It's almost as if we're saying, "Make up your mind, Spirit. Which am I supposed to be, Powerless or Powerful?"

I believe the answer is that we use the process of admitting we are powerless over our addiction to become powerful. It is one of the most difficult and rewarding spiritual practices you will ever do. I have eaten my way to over 200 lbs insisting that I could control my flour and sugar addiction. I used affirmations, prayer, advanced spiritual class work, energy work, and not until I was able to admit that my intellect was powerless over some foods was I able to find relief. The good news is it didn't take too much convincing. I had plenty of evidence on the scale and with the amount of clothes in different sizes in my closet.

I think what makes us stop short of saying we're powerless over our addiction is a <u>lack</u> of faith rather than a demonstration of faith. The process of powerlessness is the process of surrender. In New Thought we are careful to be mindful that we are not surrendering to an all-powerful being in the sky that might be wrathful or try to punish or take advantage of a person who just admitted they were powerless. We are surrendering our egocentric mind (which helped us to get where we are) to pure Love, pure Compassion, pure Potentiality.

In the Talmud, a sacred text of Judaism, it is written, "every blade of grass has its own angel standing over it whispering, 'grow, grow.'" You have your divine wisdom standing over you whispering, "grow, grow." If you think you're grown already, you make your angel's work harder. Admitting we are powerless over our addiction is the signal that we are ready to grow in a different way than we've ever grown before.

Admitting that you are powerless does not make you spiritually weak, and you are not letting God or yourself down. When you speak of this Step in your heart or around your New Thought friends, do so with the conviction that speaks of someone with the power of the One behind him.

Freedom from addiction doesn't have to be a battle. The degree of difficulty directly corresponds to your resistance to surrender, to your ability to admit at a deep level that your ego self is powerless. When you surrender your personal human power, you will begin the process of uniting with the One, which is your true identity. Truly taking this Step will yield you a human relief and a spiritual power like you've never felt before.

My experience is that picking and choosing these Steps won't yield you the freedom you're look-ing for. They are built upon each other. The Four Agreements are built upon each other. The Buddha's Eightfold Path has one wisdom leading us into another, and so do the 12 Steps.

Affirmations are powerful spiritual tools, and I use them daily. If affirmations that say, "I have power over my drinking" work, great. My hat's off to you. But don't put your life on hold waiting for it to work if it's not working. Try surrendering your self-will to your Self-will, your human self to your Spiritual Self. What we're talking about here is recognizing our ego-self is powerless to the drug alcohol, or food, or shopping, or sex, or the Internet, or smoking or ...

Here is an affirmation you may want to use to GET YOU READY for the first Step. Remember, it is not a replacement for the first Step.

*Today I let go and let God. I understand
it is not I but the Spirit who gives me
the strength to understand that I am whole,
complete, and perfect just as I am.
I effortlessly surrender to Love
and Compassion today.*

Step 2

*Came to believe that a Power greater than
ourselves could restore us to sanity.*

*There is only one life and that Life is God.
It is the one Energy of all life. It is so good to know that
I live and move and have my being in the very Energy of
Spirit. I am safe in this energy to be myself. I am free to let
go of any ego- based ideas and allow the Spirit within to
guide me on my right and perfect path. It is good to simply
surrender and allow Spirit to work through me. With deep
gratitude I let go and let God. And so it is.*

If you're in a New Thought spiritual community,
you've probably already experienced the joys of
learning how the Power works in your life. My
God is an awesome God! Once we understand that

God is not an entity but an energy that is in, through, and all around us and is ALMIGHTY, we begin to have hope for our lives.

Some of us have heard this wisdom from sponsors. "You have to come to grips with two things: There is a God, and you're not it." Such a caution is based on the idea that there is a person named God in the sky and He or She alone gets the title. Our sponsors are telling us that the characteristics of the God often talked about in the scriptures of many religions include judgment, wrath, control, jealousy, and anger. The sad truth is, that many of us, while in the grips of our addiction, thought we were this kind of controlling God, trying to run other people's lives, when we could scarcely run our own. Many of you are familiar with the term, "large and in charge" that is sometimes used to describe overbearing micro-managers who are suffering from untreated food addiction. Thinking that we have to "force things to happen" in our life is the behavior of someone who is still working with a sometimey God who may or may not be on the job when we need a favor. One who doles out the good life based on worthiness, instead of a consistent God who is both the source and supply of our good. Our work is to get our unhealed past out of the way and allow things to happen by being in harmony with Spiritual Principles.

In New Thought, we've been introduced to a new definition of God. A Presence that is ALWAYS loving and compassionate and kind. Given this God of our (new) understanding, we would amend the often shared wisdom that "There is a God and you're not it" just a little to say, "There is a God and you're not all of it." We understand that while God is all of us, we cannot possibly be all of God. God is bigger than even our biggest thoughts can conjure up.

Once again, the challenge is not in coming to believe that a Power Greater than ourselves can do anything, including relieving us of any unwanted thought or behavior. The challenge is with the second part of the Step, in admitting that while under the influence of whatever, we're insane. We don't like that. After all, many of us kept jobs, became practitioners, ministers, chaplains, CEO's, attracted mates and kept them even in the worst of our addiction.

If you haven't admitted that your behavior around alcohol or cupcakes or relationships or time spent on your computer in chat rooms or with games is insane, close this book. It won't help you. Remember, insane behavior is any behavior that doesn't serve us. Anything that keeps you from experiencing your oneness with the God of your understanding is insane. Anything that keeps you from abundance in love, money, self-respect, a generous spirit, oneness with all life is insane. Anything that keeps you from knowing and demonstrating your unique gift here on the planet is an outpicturing of your insanity.

We want to pay close attention to the wording of this Step: CAME TO BELIEVE. It's a process. Sometimes we in New Thought trick ourselves by saying, "Change your thinking, change your life." It's great motivational wisdom and a nice sound byte for many of our church brochures. And it's true, but sometimes we trick ourselves into thinking it's a quick fix. You can't change your life without changing your thoughts. But it's only the beginning of the work.

Our thoughts have to stay in our mind long enough to grow into beliefs. They have to mature so that all the evidence we have in our own mind and all the evidence that we share with others (human race consciousness) doesn't throw us off. "It is done unto you as you believe." In my thoughts I believe in unconditional peace. But when someone criticizes the way I do something or people don't vote the way I want them to or I eat a package of cookies, even though I committed to giving up flour and sugar, I can't find that thought of peace. When that happens, I realize I had conditional thoughts of peace, not a belief in peace. Moving some thoughts to beliefs may take time, it takes perseverance and as the phrase, "Came to believe" suggests, a process. I love the recovery wisdom that reminds us that we came, came to, and came to believe. We somehow found the courage to walk into a 12 Step meeting. Then we "came to" from the fog following detox, yes, even the detox of trying to control other people; and finally we came to believe that a Power greater than ourselves could restore us to a life Spirit intended for us.

The process of changing our thinking and changing our life often includes the powerful tool of affirmations. With enough repetitions and affirmative prayer, and a willingness to look for evidence, I came to believe that my Higher Power could restore me to sanity. In other words, restore the connection to the Good in my life.

God, Goddess, Allah, Elohim, the Sacred Grandmother Tree can and will return you to sanity when you cultivate the belief that It can. Sometime, even the highest bottom drunks, the drunks who've not hit a terrible bottom of jail, mental hospitals, lost jobs, broken relationships, have a hard time believing we've not lost all credibility with God. But we know from our New Thought teachings that our God is not a punishing God. God's waiting for you. Stick around New Thought communities long enough and your understanding of God will change, and change, and change some more. But one thing will stay the same: This power for good that some call God is waiting for the impress of your active belief: your conscious thought.

What does this mean, "impress of your active belief?" Think of a band of energy that is always around you waiting to take form on your strongly held belief. The energy is all-powerful. Some people think of this energy as a Genie waiting for your command while others think of clay waiting for your creativity.

You can improve your active belief, the clay mold of your desire, by remembering a time before your addiction took hold. When you could get on the internet and not even think about porn sites, when you could spend a day without thinking of sugar or flour items, when you could go to a party and get through the entire evening without dancing on a table with a lampshade on your head, when you woke up in the morning with the name of the person next to you clearly in your mind. Remember, God can only do for you what God can do through you, even restore you to sanity.

Here's an affirmation to help with that impress and again, it's not meant as a substitution for Step 2.

> *Today I believe that there is a Power*
> *for Good in the Universe which is waiting*
> *to say YES to my desire to live happily*
> *and effortlessly without a drink. I speak*
> *that desire now, knowing my word cannot*
> *come back to me void. I understand*
> *that I can have a life of adventure,*
> *excitement, and love without insanity.*
> *Serenity doesn't scare me one bit.*

Step 3

*Made a decision to turn our will and
our lives over to the care of God
as we understood Him.*

*There is only One Life, One Love, One Power. That Life is
my Life now and forevermore. There is no other Power. It is
the Power that created me, lives in me, expresses through me
and as me and I am it. It is the Love I am, the Life I am and
all that I am. By my own choice I freely let go and know that
the Power that I choose to call God/Grace/Love has Its way
with me knowing It is always Good, Orderly, Direction in
expression. I mindfully choose to let this Love guide me, care
for me, protect me, lead me through the gracious expressions
of all Life. I know this is done in the Mind of God, in the
Love of God, as I let forth these words into the Law of Mind
in Action which is also God, which acts upon my word, as
God and makes it manifest before the words have finished*

falling from my lips. I am so grateful, I am so blessed. I am
so full of the Love of God/Grace/Love. And so it is.

Wrapping your head around this Step will be made much easier if you take the last four words first, "As we understood Him". Fortunately for me, I have long since stopped trying to rewrite the Big Book, including the Steps. For the most part, that is. Yes, I'm with many of you who are a little weary of the Him, Him, Him when talking about God. But considering the era in which the 12 Steps were developed and the contribution to my life that Bill Wilson has made, I can deal. I have a little harder time leaving the "understood" alone. For me, it's not in the past tense. My understanding is alive and growing. My understanding of my Higher Power changes with every sober and abstinent breath I take, with every meditation, with every class I take or teach. God doesn't change, just my understanding of God. The deeper my understanding of Oneness (and I'm

pretty sure I've just scratched the surface) the clearer I am about what my God looks and feels and
sounds like. And tomorrow I hope it will be different. I hope that for you, too. Imagine you are on one
side of a window with a roller shade all the way
down and God on the other. Every day you are clean
and sober and abstinent of addictive behavior you
raise the shade a little higher and behold the Love
that is on the other side.

Once we begin to envision a God that is ALWAYS
loving we can begin to start the process of turning
our life and our will over. If we can let go of the
notion that God is made in the image and likeness
of our parents or teachers or clergy who we correct-
ly feel shouldn't have control over our will or our
life, then we can at least begin the contemplation of
Step 3.

May we strive to be like six- year old Naomi
whose mother one day found her intently coloring a
picture she had just finished drawing. The images

were soft and the colors she had chosen warm and inviting. "What are you coloring?" her mother asked. Naomi replied, "I'm coloring a picture of God." Her mother, having the disadvantage of being a grown-up said, "Naomi, nobody knows what God looks like." Unphased, Naomi said, "Well, tell them to hold on because in a minute they will." That's the depth of relationship that Step 3 requires.

Would you use soft images and warm colors if you were to paint a picture of God as you understand God today? Would you be as convinced as Naomi that you know what God looks like?

Let's talk about what God's will for you really is. Simply, it's to live in harmony with Spiritual Principles or as Bill W would say, "Live life on life's terms." There is no God in the sky who cares whether you live in an ashram or go to Burning Man each year. There is no God in the sky who cares whether you are rich or poor or black or white or gay or straight or evangelical Christian or Muslim.

God doesn't have a will or a plan for Jane or Tyrell or Rojellio to be architects and Sam or Julie or Maria to be stay-at-home parents. For those people, and all the rest of us, God's will is to find harmony in our careers, relationships, health, and finances. God's will is not made evident to us in the outer forms of our lives but in the inner landscape. Sometimes it helps me to think of God's street names when I think of taking Step 3. Compassion, Love, Harmony, Joy, Abundance, Adventure, Oneness. That's the kind of God I'm turning my will and life over to.

You don't need anyone else to tell you whether you're following God's will. Your gut knows. It's often helpful to check things out with a sponsor, especially when you're new in recovery and your gut hasn't yet fully detoxed from being co-dependent to your ego.

In taking this Step with a New Thought perspective, we recognize that we aren't losing control when we turn our life and will over to our Higher Power because our Higher Power is within us. We're turning our life and our will over to our Highest Self.

One affirmation for Step 3 is:

> *Today I let Compassion, Harmony, and Love*
> *run my life. I know that God's will for me is wild*
> *and unlimited success. When evidence tells me my*
> *ego has taken back the reins, I gently return*
> *my will and life to God.*

Step 4

*Made a searching and fearless moral
inventory of our lives.*

*In this holy moment, I recognize One Life, the Life of God.
It is the reality of everything I see, feel, touch and experience. All of Life is the expression and experience of the One
Life. It is perfect. It is whole. It is real. There is nothing that
separates me from the Infinite Life of the Universe. Nothing
about me is in any way contrary to the Nature of God. Every
circumstance and experience of my life is the expression of
Life living and breathing me. As I prepare to look with
honesty at my life, I know I am looking at the Life of Spirit.
There is no mistake about this. I am the honesty and
integrity of God. I know that the inventory of my life is the
inventory of Life Itself. Even in those circumstances where
I wish I had done something different, I recognize God as me.
I release all judgment and I look with courage and love at*

my life. From this place of courage and honesty, I give
thanks for this opportunity to stand in God and review my
life. I give thanks for every circumstance and experience of
my life. In gratitude, I release my word and I know it is
done as it is spoken. In letting go, I stand in trust and faith
and know that God, in me as me, sees with clarity, love and
tenderness. I know this is so and so it is.

L et's look first at the word "moral," so we can get the bunch out of our panties before we start. Morals are often defined by culture and time. Interracial couples wishing to marry before 1946 were out of luck in many of the states of this union. It was considered immoral in those days. Today we find it immoral that the law even existed, but lesbian and gay people face a similar ban in most states. There will be a day when we will look back on the ban on gay marriages with as much incredulousness as the ban on interracial marriages. Like it or not, it's the cultural norm. The point is Step 4 is not talking about morality in relation to geographic or cultural norms.

We're looking at taking an inventory of those times in our life when we fell short of our own sense of right and wrong. Maybe our own sense of right and wrong was instilled by values held by our family, tribe, temple, school, and nation, but they became refined as we grew in our spirituality. An honest and fearless 4th Step doesn't include what your mother, rabbi, ex, or even your sponsor thinks is wrong. It's what gives you that twinge when you think of it. If someone gives you a shout-out about a wrong you did them, give it an honest look, but remember the teachings of Don Miguel Ruiz, "don't take things personally."

Behaviors and patterns go on my 4th Step if they caused emotional, mental, physical, or financial harm to another person or to myself. I set the bar higher in Step 10, but for Step 4 I keep it to my causing emotional, mental, physical, spiritual, or financial harm to another person or myself. Some of us have serious shame behind losing our kids or stealing ideas from someone else to advance our careers.

Some of us have lied our way into jobs with made-up educations or experience. Some of us have had affairs while we were married or in a monogamous relationship and some of us have had affairs with someone who was married or in a monogamous relationship.

Once a student asked to see me with something she wanted to "get off her chest" because she was still feeling like she didn't belong in a spiritual community. Her "sin" was, while she was drinking, she had an affair with a married neighbor that produced a child who she gave up for adoption. The child would have been 17 at the time, and she wanted to find him, but she didn't feel worthy. She felt immoral. Working with spiritual principles and getting a better understanding of God as compassion and love, she was able to forgive herself, and she eventually found him. It is unlikely that this would have happened if she was unwilling to look deep into what she was trying so desperately to hide.

Step 4: Made a searching and fearless
moral inventory of our lives.

43

These are examples of big things that we've kept secret.

The smaller ones need to be brought upstairs for viewing as well. I once showed up at my father's hospital room drunk and it went in my 4th Step inventory. I was unable to be present with him as he went through recovery from a serious heart attack and that hurt both of us. It did not meet the standard of morality for me and had to go on my 4th Step.

So, putting "moral," in a spiritual, not religious perspective, let's move on to the rest of Step 4. Made a searching and fearless moral inventory of ourselves.

There are a number of ways to do this inventory. I've used many and they all work. The Big Book is my favorite but recently I've checked out many on the Internet that are formatted to make this very simple (notice I didn't say "easy") to accomplish. Check them all out, and find one that works for you and your sponsor. Beware of perfectionism here.

You are on a journey, and if you stay clean, sober, and abstinent, you will have lots of time.

The value of this Step is enormous. Without getting too woo-woo, your energy will vibrate at a much higher level after completing Steps 4 and 5. You have memories and even conclusions that you've drawn from your memories that need to see the sunlight of the Spirit for you to get well. This Step is designed to bring them up and get them out.

My first Foundations of Spiritual Principles teacher, Rev. Karyl Huntley, asked us to imagine an iceberg and I invite you to do that now. The iceberg, represents all the thoughts (including those thoughts about actions and events) in your mind. Seven- eighths of the iceberg is under water, leaving one-eighth above the water. Seven-eighths of your thoughts are below your conscious awareness, leaving them to do the majority of the driving of your life without your permission. A great deal of what we did under the influence is shoved down there so we won't hurt so much.

The purpose of the 4th Step is to get those thoughts from that unconscious space to our awake and aware mind so that we can let them know we are removing our permission for them to be unsupervised in our consciousness, not to make them vanish but to disempower them so our Higher Power, our Higher Self, can be fully alone in the driver's seat. We still believe in the wisdom that encourages us to "not regret our past nor wish to shut the door on it." In fact, we understand that there is tremendous spiritual growth potential in this very Step. Marianne Williamson once wrote, "The Great Spiritual Masters don't have anything we don't have. They have perfect love inside and so do we. The difference is, they don't have anything else." The 4th Step is Recovery's way of getting rid of the anything else: fear, isolationism, jealousy, victim mentality, not-enoughism, and whatever else might begin to appear when we inventory our patterns and behaviors.

Here is a spiritual teaching that will assist you in taking a strong 4th Step: All people, without excep-

tion, are always working with the very best consciousness they are able to access at any given
moment. Don't think this lets you off the hook of
consequence. It simply explains how you got wherever you are. In other words, if you could have done
better, you would have. Most of what you will
uncover in your 4th Step will turn out to be behaviors that, in that moment, made you feel safe. You
didn't know yet that other people, places, and things
could not make you feel safe or unsafe. Only conscious contact with your Higher Power can make
you feel safe, and your Higher Power is with you all
the time in all the spaces that you occupy.

Becoming unified with all the compassion that is
within you will make taking the 4th Step easier and
your learning will deepen. When we are steeped in
a consciousness of compassion, we are much better
equipped to be fearless. We need to let go of the idea
that our patterns and behaviors are sins that are to
be punished. New Thought teachings remind us
that the word "sin" is an archery term meaning "to

miss the mark" from the Aramaic language of Jesus. We embrace the notion of being fearless because we know that the deeper we can go into our old behaviors, the deeper we can know the God within.

Borrow from the Buddhist prayer before you begin the 4th Step, and stand in front of a mirror and say, "May you be filled with loving kindness. May you be well. May you be peaceful and at ease, and may you be happy." Say it six times before you begin. Keep looking in the mirror. Yes, for the entire six recitations.

Using one of the formats for Step 4, make the list of your actions and behaviors that caused harm. Will listing them change them? No. They are done. That non-specific uneasiness we all feel sometimes can come, in part, from trying not to think about the harm you caused someone else or yourself. It is like gum on the bottom of your spiritual shoes, and it is slowing you down, making it much more difficult for you to walk with God.

Here is an affirmation for Step 4:

> *Today I am compassionate with my history.*
> *I know I am a whole, complete, and perfect*
> *spiritual being having a human experience.*
> *I look at my history with the understanding*
> *it has great news for me in having a closer*
> *walk with my Higher Power, my Higher Self.*

Step 5:

Admitted to God, to ourselves, and to another human being the exact nature of our wrongs.

A PRAYER FOR STEP 5

I turn my eyes to the Great One that is in all, through all, and everywhere present. This Great one, my Higher Power, is all-knowing, all-giving and all-loving. So, in This One I am completely safe. I acknowledge that I have adopted some beliefs and behaviors that I previously thought would sustain me. But now, I am done with these. The shame that has bound me because of these beliefs and behaviors no longer holds dominion over me. And because I am thoroughly safe in The One, I can live transparently and openly, admitting those things that once bound me, and which I now leave behind.

My gratitude is unlimited for the release I am experiencing,
for the comfort of the love that surrounds me, and
for the fellowship of the free. I release this word into the
hands of the Mighty One and the never-failing Law.
I take my hands and attention off of how God does
the work, and simply let it be done.

I have yet to meet one person who hasn't felt lighter after taking this Step. You've heard the spiritual wisdom that we are only as sick as our secrets. For those of us who do not believe in a God in the sky with a notebook of our sins, our work is to know that we are admitting the exact nature of our wrongs to Compassion, Love, and Wisdom. Our God looks at our mistakes as necessary course corrections for which any punishment has already taken place as cause and effect. We are punished "by" our sins, not "for" them.

The healing juice of Step 5 is in admitting your wrongs. This is the action of removing some of the memories and thoughts that are locked in your subconscious, that part of your mind that is seven-eighths below the iceberg and saying them aloud. It is the action of moving closer to taking 100% responsibility for your life. It is the action of moving closer to understanding the spiritual meaning of the phrase, "It is not I but the Father (Indwelling Wisdom) who doeth the work." It is not your history, or your ego-based activity that will bring you a life of joy, but your union with Spirit. Admitting your wrongs will clear out those boulders that are blocking your spiritual path. And for that, we need human help.

I once heard of a story of a small boy who, while walking along a rocky river bed with his dad, said, "Daddy, I bet I can move this boulder, even though it looks too big for me. Do you believe I can do it?" The Father replied, "Son, I know you can." The boy pushed and pulled and laid on his back and tried to move it with his feet and finally he started to cry. "Daddy, I can't do it." His father asked him if he had used every resource he could find to move the rock, and the boy said, "Yes, I used my hands and feet and all my strength. There's nothing left." "You're wrong, son. There is one thing left," the father replied. "There is me. You didn't ask me for help, but if you let me help you, you can move that rock."

There is help for us in completing the 5th Step. Once we have admitted to ourselves, and our Higher Power the exact nature of our wrongs, it's time to find someone to help us by admitting our wrongs to them. Don't be afraid to interview folks. In most 12 Step Recovery programs you are free to use your sponsor or not. AA's 12 Steps and 12 Traditions tells us, "This person (with whom you share your 5th Step) may turn out to be your sponsor, but not necessarily so." I have had sponsors who had what I wanted in the way of commitment to sobriety and abstinence and their drill sergeant approach to recovery was just what I needed at the time. I was quite sure my first AA sponsors, one of whom really was a WAC (Woman Army Corp) popular in WWII, ate nails for breakfast. I chose a clergy person from another town to hear my first 5th Step.

As I matured in my recovery and my spirituality, I looked for sponsors in both my alcohol and food addiction recovery that could more easily express compassion. I found them. While these sponsors have a commitment to the 12 Steps and their consistent use of the tools of the program is strong, their style of listening and feedback was more congruent with my newfound affirmative thought and speech.

The real payoff in taking an honest Step 5, not leaving anything out, is that you are no longer alone with it. Every year my spiritual community takes 40 to 60 teenagers to a wilderness camp where there is no electricity or running water, hence no showers or flushing toilets. They can't take any electronic devices-no texting, no getting plugged into rap on an Ipod, no curling irons or hair dryers (yes, I'm sure if you live in England you heard the screeches.) After a day or two of just listening to Great Mother Earth's sounds, the kids are surprisingly more willing to open themselves up. I facilitate an exercise called The Affiliation Circle in which I announce conditions from trivial to deep, which commonly happen to teens. If they have experienced that condition sometime in their life, they step into the middle of the circle. I start with things like kids of divorced parents, kids who did better than they expected in school last year, kids who have experienced racism or homophobia and move into deeper questions like who is adopted and who doesn't think their parents listen to them and then into who was molested or who wishes they didn't live with their parents and lastly, who has a secret.

The second part of the secret condition is that if Jesus, Quan Yen or Buddha was there on the land and would disappear right after they were told the secret, would they share it? Most said no. The interesting thing is the next part of the exercise is to go around the circle as many times as necessary so that any teen who wishes, can call a condition into the circle. I wish every one of you could come to see these kids. They are taking a 5th Step. They are telling their secrets. They go deeper than I could ever imagine with secrets from their lives. This year, the day after the affiliation circle, a 14 year-old girl came to me and said, "Rev. Georgia, I have one more secret to get out, can we do the affiliation circle again? Excavating our history so that it is witnessed is powerful.

A friend of mine in recovery says her mind is a dangerous neighborhood to go in alone. Invite someone in with you, and together you will be able to do what you could never do alone; experience freedom from guilt and shame.

An affirmation to do BEFORE, but not instead of, Step 5.

Today I keep firm before me the understanding that God is all there is. The person I have chosen for my 5th Step expresses her or his divinity, especially Compassion and Infinite Wisdom. She or he sees who I am: a divine emanation of the One.

Step 6:

*Were entirely ready to have God remove all
these defects of character.*

*In the Glorious God that is All that there is, I am. I claim the
perfect release that stands in the way of my perfect divine
expression as the One. I claim an open mind and heart to be
transformed by the renewing of my mind, heart and spirit.
I release anything unlike my God the Good from my
consciousness. I let go and know the Love, the Law of Mind
and action takes my word and it is done. I am so grateful.
I am so grateful for the Love that always is.*

Let's look at the spiritually charged word first,
(the word defects.) It's a word that does not
work for most of us who are trying to
use more positive language when talking about

ourselves. But, again, let's not throw the baby out
with the bathwater. Remember, the Big Book was
written in 1939 for mostly a readership of men who,
by their own admission, were pretty hardheaded.
And I have to say, when I first sobered up, words
like defect were actually helpful in waking me up to
what I was doing to my character. You can fully
take this Step by substituting the phrase "defect of
character" with many others such as: patterns
of mistakes, defenses, unconscious negative behaviors, etc. I'm going to call them defenses here.

Our defenses are those responses to life that we
think will protect us from hurt when actually they
hurt ourselves and others. Our defenses start on the
inner landscape and are anything unlike love. In
other words, neediness, jealousy, victim mentality,
not-enoughism, people pleasing, dishonesty and
many more that are unique to you. Most often,
while our defenses start on the inner, they have
corresponding behaviors on the outer that cause
pain to us and others: stealing, emotional and

physical moving from one place or person to another (geographics), controlling, raging, letting someone else make all our decisions for us even when we don't like their decision, to name a few.

When these thoughts and behaviors go untreated, many of us look for the easier, softer fix, i.e., alcohol, drugs, food, sex, the Internet, gambling and relationships. Step 6 is a powerful continuation in the treatment process called recovery.

How do we know what defenses we have? Most of them were caught in Step 4, but I always think another look is a good idea. There are clues all around you in how you are living your daily life.

Remember, this Step is only about getting ourselves ready to have the defenses removed. The genius of the 12 Steps is revealed in so many ways, but here especially. Losing those thoughts and behaviors that you thought were keeping you safe takes courage and willingness. There is no God in the sky who will yank your defenses from you. You have to be ready to let them go. Your higher Self and your lower self may need a little wrestling time. It's worth it and if you stay on the mat, your higher Self will pull you up.

Always with compassion, look first at the outer, the conditions of your life, and trace back to the feelings of protection that got you there. I suffer from workaholism, which, in addition to contributing to an unbalanced life, has seriously challenged my recovery from food addiction. The underlying defense is the belief that I'm not enough. The faulty behavior is that if I do more, somehow I'll be enough. Saying I'm ready for this to be relieved is easy; actually trying life as a human being instead of a human doing is quite another matter. My friend Julie would invite me to Starbucks to "hang." It made me crazy to spend an hour in idle conversation. I wanted to be producing something. A therapist once assigned me the homework of staying in my pajamas all day. It was torture.

Until I was ready to have this defense lifted, I was stuck in the frenzy. Our teaching is that there is nothing to be healed, only more God to be revealed. Once the qualities of Spirit within me are revealed to my awake mind, I will be entirely ready to have God remove all my defenses of character. For instance, in my case, I am enough without producing anything, I am enough because I'm a re-presentation of Spirit on the planet.

Affirmation to be used before the 6th Step:

I am ready right now to live a life understanding that I am whole, perfect, and complete just as I am. I'm ready to effortlessly let go of those thoughts and behaviors that no longer serve me in my unification with the One.

Step 7:

Humbly asked Him to remove
our shortcomings.

There is nothing outside the love and attention of God.
This Great One exists as all there is. The Great One is
in the morning fog that hides the sun. The Great one is in the
sun that evaporates the fog. The Great One is in all comings
and goings everywhere and in all times. And I experience
change as the movement of my Higher Power within me.
I know that I am entirely held in the heart of Love, and I am
at peace in this place. I speak my word now: as the sunshine
of The Great One is rising in my heart, the fog of those
things in which I was blind lifts, evaporates and is gone.
I speak my word now: Those things I saw as shortcomings
have been removed by The Great One and are as far as the
east is from the west. The sun is shining, and with that light
there is profound gratitude in my heart. Thankful, blessed,

*and at peace, I Step in to what is next. I offer these
declarations to the One That Does The Work. I know
that is where the alchemy of life occurs. I release this
prayer into the Law of Freedom, with great joy.*

L et's take the word "humbly" first. We sometimes run from it because we are still working off the dictionary definition of humble as
opposed to the New Thought meaning. When we
resist being humble we may still be thinking it
means we have to be subservient to a person or idea.
This Step is not about subservience, but about freedom. To humbly act is to act in harmony with
spiritual principles. Humbly means teachable.
When I'm teachable I ask Him to remove my shortcomings. It's like swimming downstream with the
current instead of swimming upstream fighting
against the current. One who is humble acknowl-
edges that he or she has room for more wisdom.
Acting humbly has nothing to do with being a door-
mat. It has nothing to do with piety. It has nothing
to do with making ourselves small. It has nothing to

do with not taking credit for jobs well done. It has nothing to do with asking God in a "polite" manner. It has everything to do with our willingness to leave room in our mind for more Divine Wisdom.

The Buddhists have a wonderful story to help us stay mindful of the humble state.

"A young Samurai swordsman entered the house of a famous Zen master. He looked at the master, bowed and said, 'Master! I have reached a deep level of Zen, both in theory and practice. I have heard you are great so I come here to bow to you and hope you can teach me something.' The Zen master looked at this proud young man. Without a word, he went into the back room and brought out a teapot and a teacup. He placed the cup in front of the young man and started to pour the tea into the cup. The tea filled the cup quickly and soon began to overflow. The young man looked at the old man with a confused expression. He said, 'Stop, master! The teacup is overflowing'. The old Zen master put the teapot down and smiled at him. He said, 'This is you. You are too full already. I cannot teach you. If you wish to learn, you must first empty your cup. Can you be humble?' "

If we can agree that humble is that state of alignment with Spirit and a willingness to learn more, then let us first identify our shortcomings and then determine which ones we are willing to let go of. Our shortcomings are simply those ideas and behaviors, those embellishments, that we think we need in order to survive, i.e., jealousy, neediness, workaholism, people-pleasing, gossip, etc; whatever shows up in your 4th Step. In spiritual terms, it may be less an asking of God to remove our shortcomings, and more an allowing of our consciousness to expand into a greater awareness of what is true. We are worthy, and have no need for shortcomings that no longer serve us.

In my life, the more I realize I am worthy to breathe air simply because I am an expression of God on the planet, the easier it is to take Step 7. When I don't need to prove myself worthy by working 16 hours every day, my shortcoming of being a human doing (workaholic) instead of a human being, simply falls away. The New Thought method of asking is revealing my spiritual magnificence and consciously letting go of those behaviors that cover me up. The deeper the inner revelation that I am God, (I am not all of God, but God is all of me), the easier it is to release the shortcoming. I no longer need it.

Your shortcomings return when you are out of alignment with your spirit, when you are not being authentic. Instead of dealing with the results of your shortcomings, try for a week to welcome in the qualities of God that you want to express more of: compassion, abundance, love, creativity, self acceptance, and joy, etc., more God to be revealed.

While a spiritual foundation of our teachings is that God is within, we want to remember that God is without also. God is everywhere. Sometimes we need to ask a God outside of ourselves to remove our shortcomings in those moments when we are feeling particularly weak. When we have those moments of incomprehensible demoralization or quiet desperation we may not be able to locate the God within. God is there, but we may not be able to locate It. We try not to neglect our spiritual work to the point where we reach such states, but sometimes, when we're hungry, angry, lonely, and/or tired it can happen. We simply can't feel the God within. Our training and intellect tell us God is there, but we can't connect. Remember, the innermost God and the outermost God is the same God. There are times when I ride in my jeep and scream, "God, you need to take away this fear or hunger or remorse!"

We need to keep in mind that at some point we will have to return to the understanding of the God within, because God can only do for us what God can do through us.

And then, as spiritual teachers remind us, "expect it to happen." Look for clues that you are making headway with the release of your shortcomings. Step 7, like all the other Steps, is a spiritual practice. Keep practicing.

Affirmation for Step 7

Today I remind myself that God can only do for me what God can do through me. I speak my word of intention that the Spirit within reveals more wholeness in my life. I allow my shortcomings to go back into the nothingness from which they came

Step 8:

Made a list of those persons we had harmed and became willing to make amends to them all.

A PRAYER FOR STEP 8

*I turn within to the Power and Presence of all Life.
By knowing that I am completely connected to this Power
and Presence, I am able to let go and forgive myself, and all
others. As I forgive, I heal myself, and those around me.
Forgiveness frees me to be more than I ever thought I could
be. I am right now a wonderful instrument of divine change
and love. With thanksgiving and gratitude I release this to
the Divine Law of Mind and let it be. And so it is.*

This is a very powerful Step for those of us who study the teachings of masters that remind us that everything on the visible must first begin on the invisible. Jesus said that it is done unto us as we believe. Buddha taught that everything flows from Mind, Ernest Holmes, author of Science of Mind and founder of what is now called The Centers For Spiritual Living, wrote, "change your thinking, change your life." Making a list and becoming willing is signaling the Universe that we are serious about our wholeness, about our recovery. Step 8 invites us to change our thinking about people, including ourselves, who we have harmed. We stop hiding from them. We take them out of that area of our subconscious, dust them off, and put their names on a sheet of paper to consider becoming willing to say we're sorry for the wrong we've done to them (and to ourselves in the process). In this Step we are putting our intention for peace into the law.

I tell my congregation every Sunday morning that "everything in our experience is either a call for love or an expression of love. No exceptions."

I make my eighth Step list with this in mind. The people I have harmed most often were harmed because of my misguided attempt at finding love. If I gossiped about someone, I was trying to build myself up and make myself look more lovable with some pitiful attempt at making someone else look less than. If I stole from someone, it was because I thought that having this thing or idea would make me more lovable (even if only to myself). If I was unfaithful in my marriage, it was because I thought I needed more love than I was getting at home. None of these behaviors were ok, but understanding I was calling for love brought greater compassion. This notion, that everything in my experience is either a call for love or an expression of love has made it much easier to make a more complete list, and has been a great asset in finding a willingness to make amends. As we are taught in recovery, the mistake I made is what I did, not who I am.

Maybe you stole from people, or maybe you gossiped about them. Maybe you betrayed them when they needed you to stand up for them. Whatever the trespass, remember the powerful message of inclusive spirituality: You were working with the very best consciousness you had at the time. That teaching is not there to let you off the hook; it's there to put what you did into perspective. You still need to make amends. That person still needs to go on your list. If you could have done better, you would have. Every time.

It may be helpful to list a person and write your name on the same line after their name. You can't hurt someone else without hurting yourself. We know from our teachings that there is only One of us really, and when you injure an incarnation of that One, you've injured all within the One, including yourself.

Is there anyone who should not go on your list? Yes, there are those people who have been hurt by your actions, even though you acted honorably. Maybe someone is hurt because you got a promotion that they wanted. Maybe someone was hurt because they had to be left off a guest list due to space. Not every time someone is hurt by your actions do you need to make an amends.

My friend Jason wanted and needed to leave his wife of 27 years. They had developed separate interests and desires over the years, and he was suffocating. He wanted to travel now that the kids were living on their own, and she didn't; nor did she want him to go alone, or with a group. She found great spiritual comfort in an evangelical Christian church and he found spiritual comfort in being in nature with his fishing pole and at AA. He loved to read, and she wanted him to watch TV with her. They pretty much had stopped talking to each other and were living parallel lives. He left her without making her bad, or wrong, or not enough. He was generous with the financial separation. He didn't have anyone with whom he was having an affair. Of course she was hurt. It wasn't what she wanted. But he had done no wrong, no amends to make. Eventually, she was able to see the wisdom in Jason's actions and is now happily married to someone in her church and Jason is off somewhere in Australia having a walk-about.

As with all the 12 Steps, we want to remember that these are powerful spiritual practices for those of us who have been in recovery for some time. Set a time, maybe at the first of the year, maybe the day after your birthday, to sit down and make a list of all persons that your unconscious behavior might have hurt in the last year. Remember, this is only a list. You still have time to erase their name, but if they stay, you are making a commitment to become willing to make amends.

Willingness is one of the most powerful spiritual practices of faith that we can muster. If we really believe that God has done God's job, and the table has been set before us to choose our good, then the only thing holding us back is our lack of willingness to reach out and take what we want. One of the ways to dismantle the wall of separation between us and our Good is through this practice of listing all persons we've harmed through our addiction.

Affirmation for Step 8

I effortlessly allow the names of those I've injured by my unconscious behavior to flow onto the paper that is now before me. I welcome the opportunity to see my Oneness with them more clearly today.

Step 9:

Made direct amends to such people wherever possible, except when to do so would injure others.

I know there is one Life. There is one Power. There is one Universal Good and it goes by many names. It matters not what name it is called. It simply matters that It is. This one Life lives in all places at all times. It is the energy and power behind all things. I know that I am one with Life. It is all of me and I am part of It. I am one with love and understanding. I am one with balance and harmony. I am one with God. As I know this truth, I know that God is at the center of all amends. Every thought and every conversation is the conversation of God. I am never separate from the loving, forgiving power of the Divine. As I make amends to those I have harmed, I know the goodness of God goes before me and makes all things new. I am centered in God with every

person I make amends to. I trust God in all things and
I trust God right now. I am centered, honest, humble and
real. My heart is the heart of God and it is from this place of
my heart that I make amends this day and every day. I am
so grateful for the opportunity to walk with God this day.
From this place of trust and willingness I let go and let God.
I stand in faith and trust and I know all is well. I gratefully
release this prayer and know that it is so. And so it is.

I once went to a Buddhist retreat on forgiveness and the teacher recommended that when we returned home we go to the grocery and buy a sack of potatoes. He then suggested that we pour them out on our kitchen table and write the name of any person we had harmed on a potato and return it to the sack. When we had finished we were told to carry it around with us everywhere we went, everywhere. If we went to the store, it came with us, if we went on a date it came with us, if we went to visit with family it came with us. It sat on our desk at work. We could only remove the potato if we had admitted to the person, whose name was on the potato, the exact nature of our wrongs and said we were sorry. Soon, any potatoes left in the bag would have green shoots sprouting and eventually the potatoes left in the sack would become rotten and begin to decompose. That's what's happening to your insides.

We drank and ate and gambled and visited porn sites to keep us from smelling our own decomposition. Step 9 is not about anyone else. If they are blessed by it, thanks be to God, but this is so we can return to wholeness, back to a greater understanding of who we are.

Many of you have heard the golf joke about the two foursomes who were going to meet up at the 19th hole (the bar) after the round and when the second foursome took forever to get there, the guys in the first foursome asked what took so long. Panting, one of the second foursome replied, "Well, Charlie had a heart attack and it took longer because we had to hit the ball and drag Charlie, hit the ball and drag Charlie…" That sounded like me before

I took Step 9...I took a swing at life and dragged along all the people I had hurt because they were deep in my consciousness, giving me that uneasy feeling of impending doom. It was slowing down my spiritual walk considerably.

Of course, I have heard the spiritual wisdom that my "victims" had drawn the experience of my injury to them for the purpose of evolving their souls. And I believe this wisdom to be true. I was, perhaps, a great teacher for them, but I damaged myself in the meantime. These Steps are never about anyone else.

The tricky thing about Step 9 is knowing when to approach someone we had harmed and when not to. In one of my advanced Spiritual Principles classes, the curriculum called for students to visit a 12 Step program of their choice. One woman actually said she'd have to leave the class before attending "one of those meetings." When I asked her why, she said "one of those people" showed up at her door with an amends because "that person" passed her over for a promotion because she simply didn't like her. I'm sure it felt good for the recovering supervisor to get it off her chest, but it re-injured my student.

The genius of this Step is not only in creating a spiritual practice of taking responsibility for our past actions and saying we're sorry, but in the concept of living amends. Living amends is the action of treating people, places and things with a new respect and understanding of Oneness. Our spiritual teachings of New Thought tell us that we can change our thinking and change our lives. That's what Step 9 is about. We can talk a good game of being sorry and having changed our sorry ways, but it's the walk that counts.

I believe that Step 9 is responsible for more reconciliation between family and friends, and divorced parents who share children, than any other spiritual or self-help practice on the planet. Just last week, in preparing students for doing a vision board workshop, I asked participants to go within and remember something good that happened to them in the last year. One woman said she recently made a 9th Step to a friend she'd been estranged from for five years, and they haven't stopped talking since.

Affirmation for Step 9

Today I anchor myself in the understanding that all beings are reflections of myself. I put myself in the shoes of the ones on my list and feel what it would be like to receive an apology from me.

Step 10:

Continued to take a personal inventory and when we were wrong, promptly admitted it.

I acknowledge and recognize there is one Life. It is the Life of God. Everywhere I stand, I stand in the presence of God. Everything I do I do in the heart of God. Everyone and everything I see, feel and touch is the out-picturing of the Divine. In knowing this truth, I know that I am one with this Life. From moment to moment, I am the expression of the goodness of Spirit. I accept this about myself and about everyone now. As I accept this truth of Life, I know that every act and every word is the expression of Spirit. Everything I notice about myself is infused with the life of God. Even those things I look upon and wish I had done differently, I recognize as the awesome power of God. When I notice something I want to make amends for, I turn to the guiding power of God and Step easily, willingly and

freely into the activity of making that amend. I know that
God is in every Step and every word and every attitude.
I accept the healing power of the Divine through the action
of taking responsibility in my life. This is the power of God
living through me and as me now. I give thanks for this
awareness and for the action of making amends. I am grate-
ful for the opportunity to know and feel God's healing power
through the activities of the twelve Steps. Life is good and
I give thanks for that. I release my word into the law of
action and I accept health, wholeness and freedom now.
As I stand in the faith and the guidance of the Divine,
I know peace. I let go and I allow God and so it is.

This can become a powerful daily practice to add to your spiritual kit bag along with prayer, meditation, visioning, journaling, and service. It takes minutes and can be done while you're getting ready for bed. It's a shower for our mind.

The first nine Steps were about cleaning ourselves up, both in what we did under the influence of alcohol, drugs, food, sex, and the Internet and what we thought about ourselves and others.

Through the first nine Steps we learned the New Thought teaching that we are not victims here. Even those of us who had parents from hell started to realize we're not children anymore and we can let go of the useless activity of finding out who is to blame for our troubles. We have to give up the notion that we never learned how to do and think right. That was then and this is now. You and I have the greatest foster parents in the world in the 12 Steps and 12 Traditions. Telling ourselves, and others, that we have "taken" the Steps suggests we are willing to be called to a higher vibration. It means we're willing to "be" the attraction, not the promotion we talk about.

As the movie The Secret became popular, even those of us who were not yet students of the Law of Cause and Effect began to realize that the way we were thinking or acting in the world was creating more of the same. The hustle mentality might bring us a few more drinks but it wasn't going to bring us abundance and trying to manipulate relationships wasn't going to bring us self-respect. We had attracted many of the sorry situations in our lives from our patterns of behavior that we had developed to make us feel safe or prosperous or lovable. In Step 4 we began to identify some of these patterns, and in Steps 6 and 7, we started taking action. We set our intention to allow Spirit within to remove our defects, our cuckoo ways of operating, but often we take them back because we're scared or we haven't figured out yet how to live without them.

These patterns can't be broken simply with intention, although, they can't be broken without intention either. They need more. Our negative patterns need vigilant observance and daily interruption. It's why we call it spiritual practice. Step 10 is a daily spiritual practice that enables us to keep from needing to put more potatoes into our sacks.

Step 10 not only asks us to inventory our negative thoughts and actions, but to notice our improvement as well. It's very liberating to recognize you're not the same person as you were before working the 12 Steps. Too often we're wandering around forgetting we've changed. It's like having a right size body after recovery from food addiction but still seeing and thinking of ourselves as fat every time we look in the mirror.

Frequently, it's our family and friends who can't recognize the change. Depending on how much damage we did to their trust in us, it may take some time for them to believe we've cleaned ourselves up. I was once very active in "left" politics, what my father used to call the "lunatic fringe." I was angry at the injustices that were still facing people of color, farm workers, gay people, and what my friends and I called the "war-machine." Then, quite by accident and for all the wrong reasons, I Stepped into a Religious Science (known now as a Center For Spiritual Living) church where Rev. Mary Murray Shelton come to the pulpit and I heard the most amazing Truths that spoke to my heart and soul, even though my mind was still screaming, "religion is the opiate of the masses!" Fortunately, my heart and soul won out, and I kept returning to that church. I sat in the back row crying week after week. Once I got that we are all One, and that there were no enemies because there were no "others," I changed. But many couldn't see it for years. They forgot I was a movie not a snapshot. They tried to hold me to old ideas and old behaviors that no longer served me. I had to use Step 10 to keep myself current with who I was.

It's important that every day, as we take Step 10, we congratulate ourselves for "intuitively knowing how to handle situations which used to baffle us." It may be helpful to take one day a month, perhaps the first of each month, to get out your Big Book and review pages 83/84 to see how the "extravagant promises" are now a daily part of your life. Notice how you've changed, give thanks for it, and set your intention for more changes.

What we turn our attention to grows, and when we see the evidence of the promises of the program in our life, our good will continue to grow as well.

Affirmation for Step 10

*An inventory of today's thoughts and actions
flows easily and effortlessly through me. I remember
to notice both the things I want to let go of and the
things about myself that I want to see more of.*

Step 11:

Sought through prayer and meditation to improve my conscious contact with God as we understood Him, praying only for knowledge of His will for us and the power to carry that out.

A PRAYER FOR STEP 11

This is the place of Omnipresent Good.   This presence of Love is all that exists. God is Love, Divine Life, Principle, the all-knowing Mind. I am God's Divine idea, a place where Spirit shines through and expresses.   I am never separate and always connected, always and divinely guided.
As I seek God in the stillness, I simply let my requests be known and become still and listen, I am lead and guided by this all-knowing Mind, the place of all wisdom that knows my requests before I ask.   It is at that moment that I surrender to Infinite good, which is God's only intention

for my journey, my life.   This is my conscious contact with
God within me.   It is in this place that I recognize whole-
ness, the place where I say yes to God, and God says yes to
me. I am so grateful, and I rejoice in this revealed truth of
wholeness and strength.   I release my Word into the Law
of Love, knowing that all is well.   And so it is.

Since most of us who have picked up this book have developed a God of our understanding with whom we have already developed a relationship, this Step is now a part of our daily spiritual practice. Or at least our intention to pray and meditate each day is present. We already understand that we are a part of the omnipresent and omniscient Presence. We understand that being successful in any area of our life requires us to "hook ourselves up" to our Higher Power each day. As Dr. Michael Beckwith says, "If we make the connection, the corrections will take care of themselves." Not by magic but by design. The Universal Mind, which is located in our Highest Self, will give us all the answers we want and need. But HP won't

Step 11: Sought through prayer and meditation to improve   95
my conscious contact with god as we understood Him, praying only
for knowledge of His will for us and the power to carry that out.

force the information on us. We have to be willing to
listen. And it's hard to listen when the radio or TV is
on, when the kids need attention, when we're
rehashing a difficult conversation in our mind or on
the phone with our posse. We need to give God a
minute of our time.

When we say that God is omniscient, we mean
there is nothing that is unknown to Spirit: cures for
HIV/AIDS, cancer, war, domestic violence, stalled
creativity, how to stay out of chat rooms or our mate's
behaviors, more harmony with your teen, it's all
known to God.

We have been looking for solutions to our prob-
lems for so long in bottles, needles, rolled up in
paper, cupcakes, pornography, etc. that we forget the
solutions are right inside of us. I'm reminded of the
Muslim story about the teaching character, the wise
fool Nasruden. On one occasion, the Mula Nasruden
was outside his house crawling on his hands and
knees, searching the ground. A friend happened to
pass by and, on seeing him, asked, "Nasruden, what

are you doing in the dirt under this hot sun?"
Nasruden answered without looking up, "I have lost
the key to my house, and I am looking for it." The
concerned friend immediately offered his assistance.
'Here, let me help you. Where did you lose the key?'
"I lost it inside the house," replied Nasruden "But if
you lost the key in the house, why are you looking
for it out here?""Well, it's dark inside the house, so
I came out here to search where the light is better."
Sometimes it's easier to look outside of ourselves,
but it's never as effective.

Looking inside for the answer from our Higher
Power does not mean "what we think." Like in the
first Step, we're not talking about our ego-mind,
we're talking our Divine Mind. Where is the Divine
Mind located? It is located everywhere, both inside
and outside of you. As Ernest Holmes wrote,
the innermost God and the outermost God is the
same God.

The process of finding what we want such as
sobriety, abstinence, or freedom from any other

Step 11: Sought through prayer and meditation to improve   97
my conscious contact with god as we understood Him, praying only
for knowledge of His will for us and the power to carry that out.

addiction, starts with locating our thoughts that are aligned with Spirit. Those thoughts are best located in the stillness. Spirit is broadcasting to us all the time and we need to be on the right station. And by "right" I don't mean morally right by religious rules of right and wrong, but by doing what is in harmony with your individualized spirit. The right station that is free from the static of background noise, like TV or children or animals needing attention, will provide all the information and courage you need to get and maintain sobriety. There will be more work to do to anchor sobriety into our daily lives, but success always begins with thought. Give it time. Give it quiet.

If you do not presently have a spiritual practice of meditation, start with five minutes and begin to work up. If it doesn't work to close your eyes in the beginning, don't. You don't need to sit cross-legged on a little pillow all twisted up like a pretzel, either. Find a comfortable spot and sit in an open position. Read a daily guide from the many offerings available, either from the Recovery community or the spiritual community and then listen in the stillness for a few minutes.

Julia Cameron, in her book The Artist's Way, describes this process of creating something from nothing as taking dictation from the Divine. Creating a life of sobriety requires us to take dictation from the Divine. The good news is that most of us who have suffered from addiction already have competence in taking dictation. We've taken dictation from unskilled parents, from religious institutions, from Hollywood, from bosses, from teachers, from our peers, from bartenders and pretty much from anywhere else in earshot.

Once we practice meditation for awhile, we begin to get familiar with how God's voice sounds to us and we can make a conscious choice to take dictation from the One, not the many. Until we're clear it's the voice of our Higher Power and not the loudest voice in our internal committee, any dictation we take down we want to check out with

Step 11: Sought through prayer and meditation to improve   99
my conscious contact with god as we understood Him, praying only
for knowledge of His will for us and the power to carry that out.

a sponsor or spiritual advisor. Find out if it sounds right. For many of us, myself included, our thinking in early sobriety wasn't much clearer than when we were in active addiction. It took a more than a minute or two to evaluate ideas with a clear head. It might take a more than minute or two to begin to recognize God's voice. It's sort of like when our best friend calls, they don't have to say their name, he or she just starts talking because we know who they are. Life gets better when we are clear it's God talking to us.

Many of us are familiar with the wisdom that suggests that meditation is listening to God and prayer is talking to God. When I think of Step 11, I silently switch the word meditation to come before prayer, so I say "I sought through meditation and prayer…" For me, it's important that I listen before I talk. I've been reminded more than once that God provided us with two ears and only one mouth so that we could listen twice as much.

First, let me say that all prayer is helpful. Affirmative prayer, recited prayers from sacred scriptures such as the Bible or the Quran and modern texts such as the Big Book, posture prayers such as bowing to the east, letters to God, and screaming at God when you are up against the wall, are all good. I pray the rosary and often have conversations with God that some might call prayers. I recommend to those I sponsor to share their gratitude list as prayer. The God within likes to hear the good news too.

For those of us in New Thought spiritual communities, however, our prayer of choice is affirmative prayer, sometimes called Spiritual Mind Treatment. All of the prayers at the beginning of each chapter are examples of Spiritual Mind Treatment. Their focus is simply to open our hearts and minds to the Spiritual Truth that God has given us everything God will ever give us. The ball is in our court and prayer helps us to catch it. What we are wanting to experience in our lives may be new

Step 11: Sought through prayer and meditation to improve 101
my conscious contact with god as we understood Him, praying only
for knowledge of His will for us and the power to carry that out.

to us, but it is not new to the Universe. It's been here all along, in unlimited quantities. A good book to help better understand Spiritual Mind Treatment is called, Five Steps To Freedom: An Introduction To Spiritual Mind Treatment by John Waterhouse.

Prayer of any kind helps with the "hook-up" that is necessary for sobriety and abstinence. We don't need to wait for the 2x4 to hit us before we remember to pray. We can be proactive and set time each day for prayer and meditation. Folks in one form of the 12 Steps for food addiction are "required" to sit in the stillness for 30 minutes each day before they call their sponsor. While it can take awhile to get through the discomfort of 30 minutes of stillness, participants report a major shift in conscious contact; and taking dictation from the One is much easier. Following a healthy chunk of time in prayer and meditation each day, we can also give ourselves little pick-me-ups during the day.

The Vietnamese Buddhist, Thich Nhat Hanh, who is a teacher to so many of us, reminds us to use everyday activities to prompt our little "hook-ups". The phone ringing, a TV commercial, a stop sign, our shower, picking up the paper from the front yard. All of those moments can be a time for a quick Word with your HP. Many of us say that putting the plug in the jug gave us a life and practicing the 12 Steps gave us a life worth living. The practice of Step 11 can make that life soar beyond your wildest dreams.

Affirmation for Step 11

Today I do my part by setting aside time for Spirit. I know that everything I am seeking is seeking me right now and I effortlessly allow it to come forth in my life. My job is to be still long enough for me to recognize it.

Step 12:

Having had a spiritual awakening as the result of these Steps, we tried to carry this message to alcoholics, and to practice these principles in all our affairs.

I recognize right now there is only one Life. It is the living Principle of the Universe and it is present everywhere. No matter what I see, feel, experience or do, all of it is an expression of Spirit. I know this means I am one with Divine Principle. It is what guides, maintains, directs and sustains me. As I know this for myself, I know if for everyone I come in contact with. Regardless of appearance, I know who or what I am looking at is Spirit in form.

In knowing this truth, then, I carry this message of the 12 Steps to anyone who seeks my help. I know as I offer help, it is God offering help. I know I cannot go

against my nature, therefore I willingly help others who are
experiencing separation through alcoholism. Through the
practice of these principles, I know God shows up and
I happily allow myself to be the vehicle through which Spirit
changes lives. As I practice the principles of the 12 Steps,
I embody all of the qualities of God and I experience joy and
peace of mind. I give thanks for this. I am grateful for the
practice of the 12 Steps of Alcoholics Anonymous.
I give thanks for my recovery and all of the ways
I experience the peace and serenity of God in my life.
I am grateful for the opportunity to help others experience
this same peace of mind. From the place of deep gratitude,
I release my word and allow the Spirit of the Living God to
express in my life. I know this is good and so it is.

If you're waiting for the sound of the blowing of the shofar, or the angels to start singing before you can admit that you have had a spiritual awakening, go immediately to the closest mirror in your home. There, you will see a miracle that is the result of working these Steps. Not reading the Steps, working the Steps.

Step 12: Having had a spiritual awakening as the result of 105
these Steps, we tried to carry this message to alcoholics, and to
practice these principles in all our affairs.

For those of us who witnessed the havoc of our
lives when we were practicing our disease, we are
screaming billboards of hope. There is no "trying"
necessary to carry the message of recovery. Just seeing us living a spiritually principled life is a giant
shout out to those still suffering. Most of us are so
happy to be living a clean and sober existence, we
make the most aggressive salespeople look pale in
comparison when sharing the joys of the 12 Steps.
We want everyone to know the rewards of our new
life and, without sponsor-supervision, we're more
than happy to tell them and tell them again, and if
they didn't hear us to our satisfaction, tell them a
third time.

Where we have to "try" to carry the message of
recovery is after the initial "honeymoon" period
wears off. We are reminded in this Step to continue
to carry the message after that post-initial recovery
period, when many of us stop going to meetings so
regularly, or at all. After our initial recovery, when
our family and friends have mercifully forgotten how

we were living in our addiction, it's easy for us to forget as well.

Some would say the forgetting is a blessing. We should be grateful and move on. Leave all that behind us. Our addiction should no longer define us. I'm not my brother's keeper. There is wisdom in all of those statements, especially the last one. But it's not your brother's keeper you should be focused on, but your keeper. The seeming paradox of "you can't keep it until you give it away" is powerful wisdom in keeping yourself spiritually healthy as well as free from the ravages of your addiction.

We need people carrying the message of recovery who are positive-thinking and positive-speaking beings who know the Truth of each and every addicted person: that they are whole, perfect, and complete just as they are. It is the process of working the 12 Steps that removes the grime from the perfection that defines humans.

Quan Yin, the Buddhist Bodhisattva of Compassion, has become quite popular in the New

Step 12: Having had a spiritual awakening as the result of 107
these Steps, we tried to carry this message to alcoholics, and to
practice these principles in all our affairs.

Thought Movement and it occurs to me that her legacy is the prototype of the 12th Step.

A Bodhisattva is one who has reached enlightenment and is ready for Buddhahood, but instead of accepting full liberation, stays behind to help others along the way. 12 Steppers are Bodhisavattas and I would encourage us to take this spiritual honor seriously.

Finally, perhaps one of the most important phrases in the entire 12 Steps is this last one in Step 12, "practice these principles in all our affairs." The 12 Steps are spiritual principles. Spiritual Principles are God's delivery method. Want abundance? God has delivered it right to your door through Spiritual Principles. Want peace? God has delivered it right to your door through Spiritual Principles. Want joy? God has delivered it right to your door through Spiritual Principles. Want to stop being judgmental with your teens? God has delivered the solution right to your door. The 12 Steps open the door so that you can see what's there.

Don't let anyone tell you (including any bozos who might still have a seat on your committee) that The 12 Steps are incongruent with the teachings of new or ancient spiritual teachers. They fit beautifully with the Spiritual Truths of all the major religions, including New Thought religions. You are powerful beyond measure and you will feel that power to the extent you can surrender to the Divine Intelligence and Infinite Love that is within you.

Affirmation for Step 12

Today I allow Spirit to work through me as I share my recovery with others. I let go of any outcome and know that my Word can never come back to me void.